Family Walks
in
Pembrokeshire

Laurence Main

HIGH INTEREST · LOW MILEAGE

Scarthin Books of Cromford
Derbyshire
1994

Family Walks Series

General Editor: Norman Taylor

The Country Code

Guard against all risk of fire
Fasten all gates
Keep your dogs under proper control
Keep to public paths across farmland
Avoid damaging fences, hedges and walls
Leave no litter
Safeguard water supplies
Make no unnecessary noise
Protect wildlife, plants and trees
Go carefully along country roads
Respect the life of the countryside

Published 1994

Phototypesetting by Paragon Typesetters, Queensferry, Clwyd

Printed by Redwood Books

ISBN 0907 758 75 4

Cover illustration by Andrew Ravenwood: *The Coast Path near Trevine (Route 5)*

The view from Garn Fawr (Route 2)

Preface

Pembrokeshire disappeared with local government reorganization in 1974. It just won't die, however and awaits promised resurrection as a county soon. It has a distinctive identity, reflecting the vitality of a peninsula made up of enchanting scenery. Here are spectacular cliffs, sandy beaches, magical offshore islands and tidal creeks. The coastline is recognised as a National Park but inland are the mystical Preselis, home of the Stonehenge bluestones. Prehistoric burial chambers and standing stones abound, while you can set foot on the ancient Golden Road. Wales glories in the 'Age of the Saints' when England suffered a Dark Age. Chief among them was St David and his cathedral has been a target for pilgrims for centuries. Much work has been done on improving the public footpaths here in the last few years. By exploring them you will introduce the family to a world well away from televisions and computer games. Enjoy the fresh air, the close contact with nature and the tranquility that inspires the imagination. Make a start with these routes.

Acknowledgements

Family camping and youth hostelling trips to Pembrokeshire were made by public transport before I started this book. We can particularly recommend the youth hostels, of which there are an encouraging number in Pembrokeshire. When it came to doing the book, I found a marvellous companion in Letty Rowan, who drove me to all but one of the walks. No sooner was the last walk done when the weather changed and snow swept the country, so Letty even managed the sunshine too!

About the Author

Laurence Main is the author of over 30 footpath guidebooks, including five other titles in the Family Walks series, covering Mid Wales, Snowdonia, Oxfordshire, the Isle of Wight and the Isle of Anglesey. He is a full-time writer and contributes regularly to walking magazines, including *Country Walking* and *Trail Walker,* plus the *Western Mail*. Married with four children, Laurence is the voluntary footpaths secretary for the Ramblers' Association in Meirionnydd, where he has lived since 1981. Born and educated in Oxford, he was a teacher in Swindon for six years before that.

Contents

Map of the area

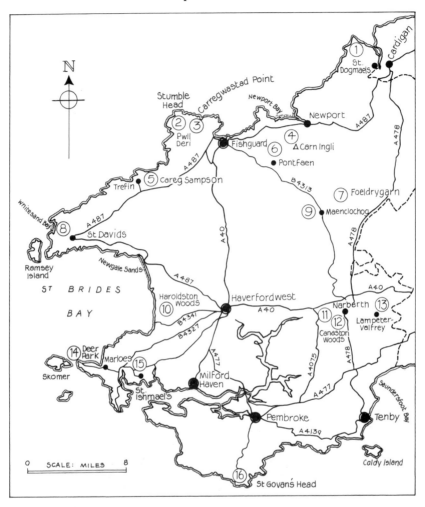

Introduction

This is a book of short, undemanding walks. Only one reaches four miles in length, but each has its own special feature to attract and stimulate young minds. This could be a cathedral or a stone circle, a stretch of magnificent coastline which once witnessed a dramatic shipwreck, or ancient woodland where you might expect to meet a druid. Buy stoneground wholemeal flour from a working water mill, meditate in a hermit's chapel, consider the course of history at the spot where the last foreign invasion of these shores was made, tread where knights rode during the Middle Ages or visit a deer park with no deer but a splendid view of an offshore island famous for its puffins. Rest your head where St Brynach communed with the angels and enter the ruins of a castle which may have been where Rhiannon was forced to do penance for a crime she didn't commit. Walk the inspiring clifftop paths, descend to sheltered beaches and admire the views from hilltops. Follow the waymarks to enter the land of mystery and magic.

Pembrokeshire's Coast Park is exceptionally beautiful. Proud cliffs defy buffeting waves. This is the only National Park that is based on a coastline. It is also less plagued by touring motorists. Do expect to meet people walking the Coast Path. These little bits of it will whet your appetite to emulate them, but those who stick to the Coast Path will miss so much inland. The Preseli Hills simply couldn't be ignored when the National Park boundary was drawn and it extends inland to include them. It is still the smallest of the parks, covering only 225 square miles.

Signpost on the walk from Carregwasted Point (Route 3, direction point 6)

In Haroldston Wood

Walking and close contact with the real, living world is an essential part of growing up, especially in the video age. Walking is a natural activity which requires little in the way of money and gives enjoyment without any competitive element. It is ideal for families, who do not need to join a club in order to do it. The Ramblers' Association have thriving local groups all over the country, including Pembrokeshire. The walking season never ends, indeed each month brings its own character and invites you to repeat a walk at different times of the year. The winter is often the best time for a short, brisk walk, as long as commonsense prevails regarding the weather.

Take care on the clifftop paths and avoid being caught out at dusk. Allow for a pace of one mile an hour. Equip your child with stout shoes and an anorak. Avoid jeans (which are very uncomfortable if soaked) and opt for several thin layers of clothing rather than one heavy jersey. A rucksack will be needed to carry spare clothes as well as your picnic, camera and maps. Make a practice of carrying the relevant Ordnance Survey Pathfinder map (at a scale of 2½″ to one mile) on your walks. The relevant numbers are given on each route map, which is drawn to an even more generous scale to show stiles, gates and other features. Older children can be taught to use a compass (and be intrigued by what happens to it at Gors Fawr and on Carn Ingli).

Symbols used on the route maps

>- >- The footpath route with direction from the start

③ Number corresponding with route directions

------ Other paths (not always rights of way)

═══ Motor road

~)├~→ Bridge

~~~→ River or stream with direction of flow

○○○○○○○○○ Wall

-*-*-*-*-* Hedge or fence

■ ■ ■ Buildings

Trees

Stone circle

○ Standing stone

✝ Church or chapel

Castle

S Stile

G Gate

Cromlech

P Signpost

O.S. Relevant Ordnance Survey Pathfinder map

Bus Bus stop

-◇- Cairn

⊏⊐ Ruin

N Direction of North (not always at the top of the map)

Each map has a scale in miles and a gradient profile showing the height in feet above sea level and the distance in miles from the start

The Ogham Stone, St Dogmael's

St Dogmael's

Outline

Post Office – Abbey Ruins – Cwm Degwel – Mill – Post Office.

Summary

The extent of the abbey ruins come as a surprise, while time should also be allowed to visit the mill. A high path above Cwm Degwel provides a taste of adventure before a quiet valley road leads back to St Dogmael's.

Attractions

Ask at the vicarage for the key to the church. At its back is a very significant inscribed stone. Dating from the sixth century, it is carved in both Latin and Ogham (old Irish). A memorial to 'Sagranus the son of Cunotamus', has helped experts decipher the Ogham alphabet.

The abbey dates from the early 12th century and by the end of the 13th century its endowments had enabled a splendid example of the free-flowing Early English style to emerge in this remote corner of Wales. Grand buildings and swollen abbey coffers swept away religious austerity, however, while the monks became notorious for indulging in Gascon wine. A crackdown in 1402 led to one of the more bibulous brethren being ordered to give his ration of wine to the poor in the abbot's presence, while the others had their wine allowance reduced.

The monks may have been the first to mill corn across the road from the abbey. Restored in the 1980s, the water-powered mill produces a range of stoneground flours, while the mill pond is home to a variety of wildfowl.

The mill and tea room are open daily throughout the summer from 10.30 am to 5.30 pm (except Saturday and Sunday morning). The mill only is open from October to Easter between 9.30 am and 5 pm on weekdays (tel. 0239 613999).

Refreshments

St Dogmael's Mill.

Route 1

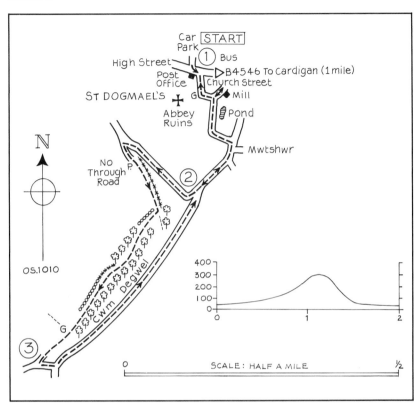

Route 1

St Dogmael's   2 miles

Start

The Post Office, St Dogmael's. St Dogmael's is one mile west of Cardigan on the B4546, on the south side of the Afon Teifi. The Post Office is near the bus stop and the car park (GR SN164460).

Route

1. *Face the Post Office in St Dogmael's High Street and go left, immediately forking right down Church Street. Pass the church and gateway to the abbey ruins on your right, then the mill pond on your left. Reach a T-junction and go right, soon passing Mwtshwr on your left. Ignore another road on your left.*

2. *Fork right along a narrow lane which is lined by houses on your left-hand side and affords a fine view over the ruined abbey on your right. Turn very sharply left to take a No Through Road which soon becomes a signposted footpath. This exciting route overlooks a valley on your left before descending.*

3. *Go left along the road in the valley floor, ignoring a turning which soon appears on your right. Continue back into St Dogmael's and retrace your steps past the pond, now on your right. Fork right to visit the mill and don't forget to visit the abbey ruins and the church, on your left, before returning to your car park or bus stop.*

Public Transport

Cardigan is easy to reach by bus from Aberystwyth (no 550), Carmarthen (nos 460, 461 and 462), Fishguard and Haverfordwest (no 412) — all of which places have railway stations. Bus no 407 runs to St Dogmael's from Cardigan on weekdays throughout the year, while no 409 runs on Tuesdays only.

13

Below Garn Fawr

Pwll Deri

Outline
Car park east of Garn Fawr — Trefasser — Pwll Deri — Garn Fawr — Car park east of Garn Fawr.

Summary
A breezy walk around a hill brings you to the dramatic coastal scenery of Pwll Deri. Climb the 678 ft (213m) summit of Garn Fawr to enjoy the views on the way back to the car park.

Attractions
Few youth hostels are as splendidly situated as Pwll Deri's, so consider staying the night here (a family room is available and the telephone number is 03485 233). The wild beauty of these cliffs has witnessed shipwrecks, with the *Dan Beard* visible at low tide at the southern end of Pwll Deri, between two tiny pinnacles at the base of a vertical cliff wall. Built as a Liberty Ship in California in 1943, its welded construction wasn't expected to last longer than five years. There was an urgent need to replace cargo ships lost to U-boat action if Britain was not to be starved into losing the war. The 7,176 ton *Dan Beard* was hit by a torpedo fired from U.1202 off Strumble Head on 10th December, 1944. The ship broke into two and 29 men lost their lives. The stern section sank in deep water but the bow section drifted ashore here. Some of the crew managed to come ashore in lifeboats, while the St David's Lifeboat rescued 12 men.

There is an excellent location for bird-watchers, especially in the spring and autumn. You should see choughs and fulmars, while grey seals used to breed here in September and October. Come in May to see the varied flora on the clifftop, with cowslips and early purple orchids blooming among the heather. Spring squill, kidney vetch and the hairy greenweed add more colour.

There is a magnificent view from the summit of Garn Fawr, emphasising the treeless, windswept nature of this rugged landscape. The rock-strewn summit bears the remains of an Iron Age fort. Look north to see Strumble Head's lighthouse.

Trefasser is an intriguing placename because it is known that Asser, the friend and adviser of King Alfred the Great, was educated at nearby Llanwnda (Route 3). The memorial stone passed on this walk is much more recent, being to the poet Dewi Emrys (1879—1952). He composed the lines: 'Athinar meddille sy'n dwad ichi pen foch ishte uwchben Pwllderi', which can be rendered in English as 'Thoughts come to you when you are sitting above Pwllderi'.

Refreshments
Bring your own!

Route 2

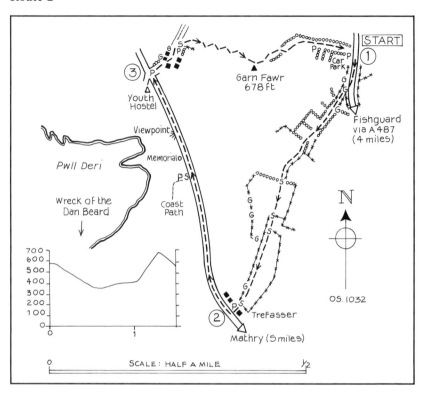

Overlooking Pwll Deri from Garn Fawr

16

Route 2

Pwll Deri   1½ miles

Start

Turn off the A487 St David's to Fishguard road. An official car park just over four miles to the west of Fishguard is on the eastern side of Garn Fawr, half a mile north of Harmony (GR SM899388).

Route

1. *With your back to the car park, go right along the lane towards Harmony. After just over 100 yards, bear right through a gate to take a sheltered path which passes a ruin on your right. Continue in this direction but avoid a cul-de-sac ahead by taking a gap immediately to its right and following the left-hand edge of a field to a stile ahead. Maintain this direction through three more fields and over three more stiles to reach a lane at Trefasser.*

2. *Turn right along this lane, walking with the sea on your left. Pass a stile for the signposted Coast Path, the memorial to the poet Dewi Emrys, a viewpoint and Pwll Deri youth hostel.*

3. *Turn right to take a signposted path through a farmyard. When it emerges as a grassy track, turn right over a stile to climb to the 678 ft (213m) summit of Garn Fawr. Continue down the other side to reach the car park.*

Public Transport

The nearest bus stops are all over four miles away, at Goodwick, Fishguard and Mathry (no 411 running between Fishguard and St David's).

The monument to Dewi Emrys, Pwll Deri

Carregwastad Point

Outline
Llanwnda − Castell − Carregwastad Point − Llanwnda.

Summary
An old lane leads to a farm called Castell which has evidence of a defensive earthwork encircling it. This was dug long before the French invaded in 1797. Reach the coast at the memorial to this farce. Return inland through fields to St Gwyndaf's Church.

Attractions
The peaceful hamlet of Llanwnda is the last place you'd expect to come across evidence of the last foreign invasion of these shores. It is a spiritual place and an old stone circle is said to have stood upon its green. The church dates from around 500 AD and is dedicated to St Gwyndaf, who probably came from Brittany. It has a Celtic bellcote tower, while there is a holy well nearby, on your right as you approach the last stile and gate of this walk. Note, too, the leper's squint in the porch. The craggy volcanic outcrop of Garnwnda, just to the south, is the site of a Neolithic burial chamber. Asser, who taught King Alfred so many of this island's secrets, was educated here, while Giraldus Cambrensis, the great 12th century traveller, was a rector here.

History has proved that French soldiers are no match for Welsh women. This fact was demonstrated in 1797, when the French believed that the oppressed peasants were ready to rise up against the English crown. To help them do this, a lugger, a corvette and two frigates slipped out of Brest on 17th February, 1797. On board were 1,400 men each with 100 rounds of ammunition and four days' rations of food and double brandy. They should have landed at Bristol but a sighting of the Dublin packet boat frightened them and they ended up here. This may not have been by chance. One of the invaders was James Bowen from a farm near Carregwastad. He had been transported for horse-stealing and either took the chance of a passage home or intended malice against his former employer. This wasn't the French Foreign Legion but the Black Legion, complete with black armbands. Most of the soldiers were convicts and their leader was an Irish-American, Colonel Tate.

Landing here by moonlight on 22nd February, 1797, the invaders soon took the heights of Garnwnda and knocked up the local farmers. They found to their delight that everybody was well-supplied with Portuguese wine from a recent shipwreck. As they drank it, the local militia was assembled by Lord Cawdor. The stars of the show were the women, whose red cloaks and hard hats (not, then, the top hats) made them resemble soldiers from a distance. Jemima Nicholas, a cobbler from Fishguard, captured 12 of the invaders with the aid of a pitchfork and by 4 pm on 24th February they had all surrendered (some paralysed with drink).

Route 3

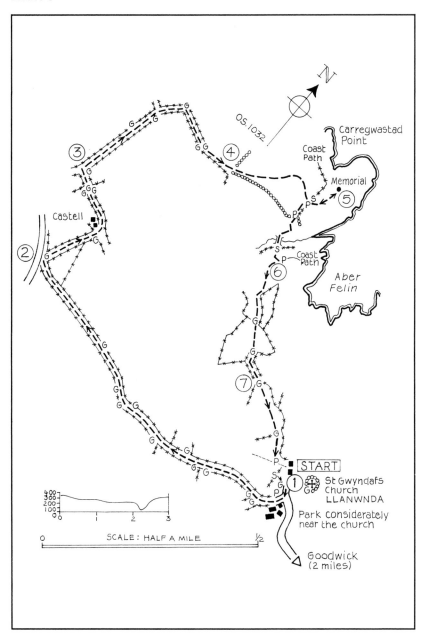

Route 3

Carregwastad Point   3 miles

Start
Llanwnda, two miles by road west of Goodwick. Cars can be parked considerately near St Gwyndaf's Church, Llanwnda (GR SM932395).

Route

1. *With your back to the church gate, take the 'road unsuitable for motors' ahead, passing the access lane from Goodwick on your left. Bear right at a fork and follow the enclosed track to a road.*

2. *Turn right immediately from the road and bear left past Castell to reach a T-junction.*

3. *Turn right and fork right to emerge from the enclosed path with the sea on your left. Go ahead along the right-hand edge of a field.*

4. *Take the left-hand of two gaps ahead so that you continue with a wall on your right. Bear left to reach a stile beside a signpost in a fence ahead and continue to the memorial on Carregwastad Point.*

5. *Retrace your steps to the stile, cross it and turn left. Take the gap ahead and bear left down to a footbridge over a stream. Cross it and a subsequent stile, then climb to a signpost at the rim of this valley.*

6. *While the Coast Path goes left, bear right, passing gorse bushes on your left. Follow a fence which appears on your left and reach a waymarked gate. Go through it and across a field to a second gate. Go ahead along an old green lane.*

7. *Continue through a waymarked gate and across a field, or around its left-hand edge, to another waymarked gate. Go ahead along a track to a signpost. Ignore a crosstrack by going ahead to a stile. Turn left over this to return to St Gwyndaf's Church, Llanwnda.*

Public Transport
Add four miles to this route to allow for the return walk from the nearest bus stop in Goodwick (service no 410 from Fishguard).

Refreshments
Bring your own!

Careg Coetan burial chamber, Newport

The 1,138 ft summit of Carn Ingli

Carn Ingli

Outline
Newport — Careg Coetan Burial Chamber — Newport — Carn Ingli — Newport.

Summary
Carn Ingli is the original mystic mountain. Its name means 'Peak of Angels' and refers to the fact that the sixth century Celtic saint, Irishman and contemporary of St David, Brynach, used to climb it regularly in order to commune with the angels. Follow in his footsteps to enjoy the view over a wide sweep of Cardigan Bay, but first pay a visit to a prehistoric burial chamber which happens to be on a ley or spirit path running through the summit of Carn Ingli and south to a cairn on Cerrig Lladron. This line passes very close to a standing stone at SN064351. The path becomes rocky and steep, while the walk starts close to sea level, making the 1,138 feet a worthy ascent. Expect a Celtic mist to descend, so pay attention as you climb to make retracing your steps easier.

Attractions
Angels are no longer fashionable. Does that mean that we should scoff at the story of St Brynach? Here your author can add a personal note based on experience. *The Ley Hunter* magazine (PO Box 92, Penzance, Cornwall, TR18 2XL) organises primary research into earth mysteries, including a dreamwork project where volunteers sleep at powerful ancient sites, their dreams are recorded and kept highly confidential so that other dreamers aren't influenced by them. If different dreamers at the same site come up with the same pattern of dreams then the actual site may be significant. Your author has been co-ordinating this dreamwork project at Carn Ingli. Unable to spoil the research by breaking confidentiality at this stage, he can report an important, vivid and powerful dream as a result of spending a night at this exposed spot in a wet November. Such dreams have to be earned! St Brynach prayed and fasted. His reward was seeing angels on a Welsh 'stairway to heaven'.

If you worship at the altar of science you may prefer to know that the jagged peak of Carn Ingli has places where a compass needle is deflected by up to 180 degrees (so that it points south when it should point north). This is because minerals in the rock were 'frozen' when the earth's magnetic poles were reversed. Magnetism may well stimulate the brain and cause altered states of consciousness. Read more about this in *Places of Power* by Paul Devereux (Blandford, 1990).

As with the prehistoric dolmen Careg Coetan, also known as Arthur's Stone, and the perceived leys or spirit paths, there is much we have still to learn on this subject. Why not spend a night here yourself?

The town of Newport, by contrast, has the imposed feel of a garrison town built around the 12th century Norman castle. This is now a private home, having been restored in the 19th century.

Route 4

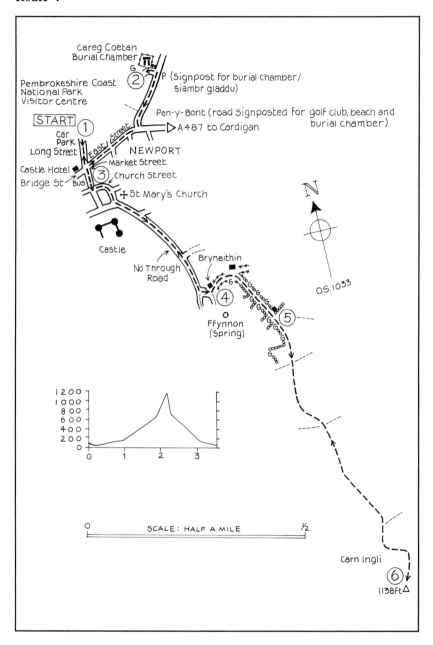

Careg Coetan Burial Chamber

Pembrokeshire Coast National Park Visitor Centre

P (Signpost for burial chamber/ siambr gladdu)

② G

START

Car Park

①

Long Street

East Street

Pen-y-Bont (road signposted for golf club, beach and burial chamber)

A487 to Cardigan

NEWPORT

Market Street

Castle Hotel

Bridge St

Bus

③

Church Street

✝ St Mary's Church

N

Castle

No Through Road

Bryneithin

④

Ffynnon (Spring)

G

⑤

OS.1033

1200
1000
800
600
400
200
0

0   1   2   3

0   SCALE : HALF A MILE   ½

Carn Ingli

⑥

1138ft △

24

Route 4

Carn Ingli

Start

Newport is on the A487 between Fishguard and Cardigan. Start from the Pembrokeshire Coast National Park Visitor Centre in Long Street, opposite a car park. The bus shelter is around the corner, facing the Castle Hotel (GR SN057392).

Route

1. *Face the National Park Visitor Centre and go right up Long Street to the cross-roads in the centre of Newport. Turn left along East Street and pass the Golden Lion on your left, then turn left, as signposted for the golf club, beach and burial chamber. Look for another signpost for the burial chamber on your right, pointing across the road to a turning on your left which you take to see Careg Coetan enclosed in a corner on your right.*

2. *Retrace your steps past the Golden Lion to the crossroads in the centre of Newport and turn left up Market Street.*

3. *At the next crossroads turn left along Church Street to pass St Mary's on your left. Fork right up a No Through Road which eventually turns left to Bryneithin.*

4. *Pass Bryneithin on your left as you go ahead along a track which bears right to climb to a gate giving access to the open moorland.*

5. *Follow a narrow but well-trodden path up to the summit of Carn Ingli.*

6. *Retrace your steps back down to Newport.*

Public Transport

Newport can be reached on weekdays by a good bus service (no 412) which runs between Cardigan, Fishguard and Haverfordwest (where there is a railway station).

Refreshments
Newport has a choice of places offering refreshments.

Pwll Whiting (Route 5)

Careg Sampson

Outline

Trefin − Coast Path − Careg Sampson − Trefin.

Summary

An impressive burial chamber with a 3-ton capstone is the icing on the cake for this marvellous walk. The clifftop path is a visual delight and as fine a stretch as any along the famous Pembrokeshire Coast Path.

Attractions

Cliffs framing the three deep bays on this route are formed of 500-million-year-old Ordovician rock. Fascinating shapes have been created by folding, faulting and the action of the waves. Seals may be spotted in the clear waters, while fulmars nest on the high rock ledges. Come in May to enjoy the carpet of wild flowers.

Iron Age Celts dug the ramparts that gave them protection on Castell Coch. The people who erected Careg Sampson burial chamber lived 5,000 years ago in the New Stone Age. The capstone was positioned by Sampson with the aid of just faith and a finger. Is this a memory of ancient powers? Sampson's name may have become attached to the monument during the period after the famous Celtic saint of that name (or spelled Samson) died in the sixth century. His little finger (with the power to raise the heavy capstone) is said to be buried on Ynys y Castell (just offshore from Abercastle). Since St Samson died at Dol, Brittany, in 565, could this be a folk memory of a spirit path from the burial chamber to the island?

Between Ynys Deullyn and Ynys y Castell lies the wreck of the *Leysian,* which (at 4,703 tons) became one of the largest steamers to hit directly into the cliffs of North Pembrokeshire in thick fog during the First World War on 20th February, 1917. No lives were lost, unlike the nine men who were killed during the wreck of the *Ragna* during a hurricane near Trefin on 27th December, 1900.

Refreshments

There is a shop, a pub and a seasonal tea room in Trefin.

Public Transport

Trefin is served by bus no 411 from Fishguard and St David's.

Route 5

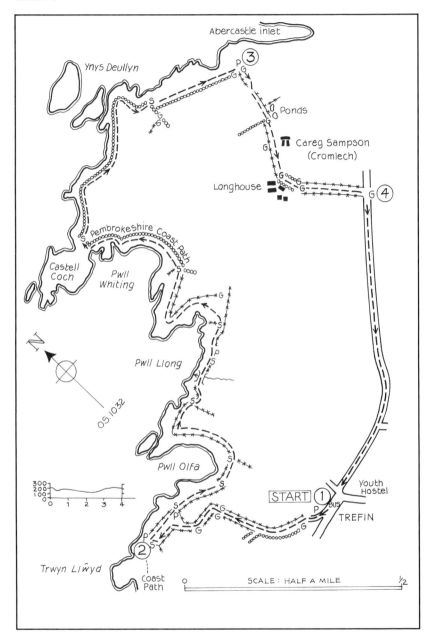

Route 5

Careg Sampson

4 miles

Start

Trefin (Trevine) lies just off the A487 Fishguard to St David's road. Start from the bus shelter in the centre of Trefin, not far from the youth hostel. Motorists can park considerately nearby (GR SM839325).

Route

1. With your back to the bus shelter, go right and bear right along a signposted footpath which begins as a metalled road. Continue to the Pembrokeshire Coast Path.

2. Turn right along the Coast Path and follow this for two miles, keeping the sea on your left.

3. As you approach the inlet of Abercastle, turn right through a gate to walk inland with a fence on your right. The path bears right over a stile to put the fence on your left. Go ahead through a gate to follow a farm track. Pass Careg Sampson burial chamber on your left. Bear left through the farmyard at Longhouse and along its access lane to the road.

4. Go right along the road back to Trefin.

Careg Sampson burial chamber

29

A wooden causeway over the muddy path in Coed Pont Faen

Pont Faen

Outline
Pont Faen – Dan Coed – Pont Faen.

Summary
This is a pleasant woodland walk, starting along the valley floor then climbing to a path which runs along the top of a wooded slope. Visit the churchyard containing the ancient stones which are linked with the bridge over the Afon Gwaun to form this place's name.

Attractions
The steeply wooded slopes of the Gwaun valley have escaped the plough and have the spirit of the ancient wildwood. Native broadleaved trees provide habitats for insects, birds and mammals, while otters survive in the river. This is the place to spot alder, ash, beech, birch, blackthorn, grey willow, hawthorn, hazel, holly, hornbeam, oak, rowan, sweet chestnut, sycamore, wild cherry and wych elm trees. Wood warbler, willow warbler, chiff chaff, wren, robin, thrushes, finches, woodcock, buzzards and ravens fly overhead. Now a designated Site of Special Scientific Interest, the wood was coppiced before the Second World War. The taller trees stand on the lower slopes, where alder and willow enjoy the damp conditions. Some beech trees are over 200 years old. The oaks and rowans near the top path are stunted by the shallow soils. Fungi abound here in the autumn. When you emerge at the roadside, go left to visit the church (dedicated to St Brynach) where two enigmatic stones stand in the churchyard. One is marked by a Latin cross, the other by a Celtic cross. They emphasise the antiquity of this river-crossing.

Refreshments
There is a pub (the Dyffryn Arms, just across the bridge).

Route 6

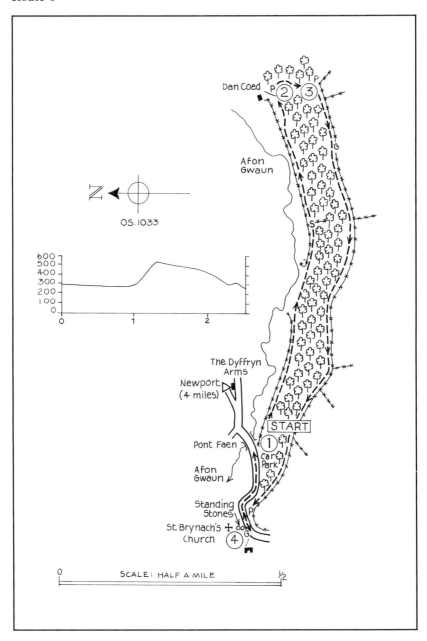

Dan Coed

P ② ③ P

Afon
Gwaun

G

OS.1033

N

600
500
400
300
200
100
0

0   1   2

S

The Dyffryn
Arms

Newport
(4 miles)

START

Pont Faen

① ③
Car
Park

Afon
Gwaun

Standing
Stones

P

St. Brynach's
Church ④ G

SCALE: HALF A MILE

0   ½

32

Route 6

Pont Faen   2½ miles

Start

Pont Faen lies about half a mile north of the B4313 road (running between Fishguard and Narberth). A small car park at the edge of woodland between Pont Faen's bridge and church is where the walk begins (GR SN024339).

Route

1. *Follow a path going from the back of the car park. The wooded slope is on your right and its boundary hedge is on your left, with the meandering Afon Gwaun beyond that. Go ahead over a stile.*

2. *Reach a Pembrokeshire Coast National Park sign for Coed Pontfaen and fork right up the wooded slope.*

3. *Reach a waymark post at the top of the slope, where there is a junction with the upper perimeter path coming from your left. Bear right along it, overlooking the woodland and the valley on your right. When you eventually come to a lane, go left along it and turn right to reach the church with the standing stones.*

4. *Return to the lane and go left to walk back down to the car park, on your right just before the bridge.*

Public Transport

There is a bus (no 343) which runs on Fridays only from Fishguard (currently at 9.30 am) to Llanychaer (Bridgend Inn) and continues to Haverfordwest before returning from Llanychaer (currently at 2.50 pm) to Fishguard. This should allow time both to walk the three extra miles each way along the Gwaun Valley to the start of this walk and for the walk itself (a total of 8½ miles). Otherwise, it's a longer walk from Fishguard, Dinas or Newport, all of which places have good bus services.

The 1,200 ft summit of Foeldrygarn

The path up Foeldrygarn

34

Foeldrygarn

Outline
Roadside west of Crymych − Foeldrygarn − Golden Road −
Roadside west of Crymych.

Summary
The enchanting Preseli Hills are so special that the Pembrokeshire Coast National Park
was extended inland to include them. Once clothed by trees and relatively densely
populated, they now offer the rambler wide open spaces. The 1,200 ft (363m) summit
of Foeldrygarn is an excellent viewpoint and easily accessible. Return along the prehistoric Golden Road. If you have the time, divert along it to see where Stonehenge's
bluestones came from, at Carn Menyn.

Attractions
There is a timeless air about this windswept moorland but much has changed since the
time that people lived here, from about 3000 BC to AD 100. The only trees now are
in a modern plantation of alien conifers. The summit of Foeldrygarn (Three Cairn
Hill) is the most intriguing place. On a clear day you can see the Black Mountains
to the east, Snowdonia in the north and the Wicklow Hills to the west, across the Irish
Sea. The hill is named after the three cairns on its summit. These date from the Bronze
Age, before the summit was enclosed by a rampart of dry stone and earth with no
ditch. Two further enclosures were added on the northern and western slopes. Hut
platforms have been found inside the enclosures along with beads and pottery from
the Iron Age and the Roman period.

A large, flat stone on the summit is called Bwrdd y Brenin (the King's Table) and
is fabled to hide a pot of gold. This may be a folk memory of this spot's importance
to the spiritual landscape. The concept that has survived in so-called primitive cultures
throughout the world was rediscovered in this country by Alfred Watkins in the 1920s.
He coined the word 'ley' and wrote about these alignments of ancient and holy sites
in *The Old Straight Track* (1925). Since then a lot of research has been done by such
as Paul Devereux, the editor of *The Ley Hunter* (PO Box 92, Penzance, Cornwall,
TR18 2XL).

Three Leys would seem to converge on Foeldrygarn. One ley, or spirit path,
connects it with Carreg Coetan in Newport by way of Pentre Ifan burial chamber.
Another goes to Mynydd Carningli and a third goes to Castell Henllys. Significantly,
five stones of this hill's volcanic ash were taken in ancient times to Stonehenge.

Nearby is Carn Menyn, which is where nearly all of Stonehenge's bluestones came
from. Suitable shapes could still be selected from similar stones on the site that have
been weathered down in a columnar form that obviated quarrying. The fact that
Stonehenge's bluestones came from here was discovered in 1923 by Dr Herbert

Continued on page 38

Route 7

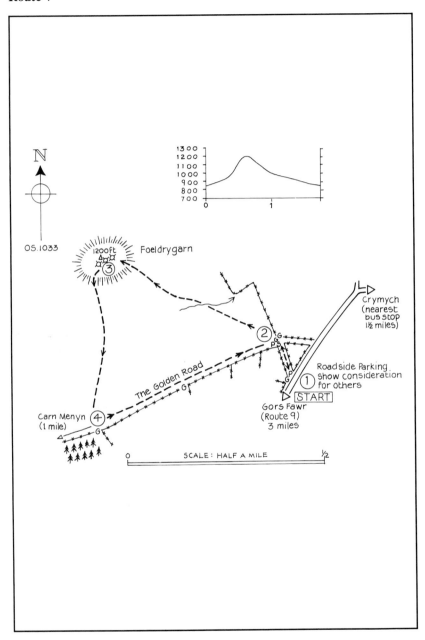

N

05.1033

1300
1200
1100
1000
900
800
700
0   1

1200ft   Foeldrygarn
③

Foeldrygarn

Crymych
(nearest
bus stop
1½ miles)

② G

The Golden Road

G

Roadside Parking.
Show consideration
for others
①

START

Gors Fawr
(Route 9)
3 miles

Carn Menyn ④
(1 mile)

G

SCALE: HALF A MILE
0   ½

Route 7

Foeldrygarn   1¾ miles

Start

Near Crymych on the A478 about 10 miles south of Cardigan. The walk begins at a parking space across the road from a signposted track just over one mile west of Crymych. If coming by bus, take the 430 from Cardigan to Crymych (tel. 0267 233 333 ext. 4333 for times). Drive or walk south through Crymych, passing the schools on your left. Take the first turning on your right and follow this road for about one mile to a T-junction where you go left for about a quarter of a mile to reach the signposted path on your right (GR SN165331).

Route

1. *Cross the road to go up the signposted track. Reach a junction with another track coming from your right. Turn left over a stile beside a gate to enter open moorland.*

2. *Bear right along the signposted public footpath that climbs to the top of Foeldrygarn.*

3. *Bear left as you descend to aim to reach the signposted bridleway (the Golden Road) at the edge of the conifer plantation to the south of the moorland.*

4. *Turn left along the prehistoric Golden Road and walk with a fence on your right back to the stile which you took to enter this vast open space. Cross it again to turn right and retrace your steps to the start of this walk.*

Public Transport

Allow nearly one hour each way to walk about one and half miles between the bus stop in Crymych and the start of this walk. It is possible, indeed enjoyable. At present Crymych is served by a bus (no 430) from Cardigan on weekdays. The 10 am departure from Cardigan arrives in Crymych at 10.30 am and the 2 pm (not Wednesdays) bus from Crymych reaches Cardigan at 2.30 pm. This allows three and a half hours for a walk of nearly five miles, time for a picnic and refreshments in Crymych. Don't come by bus on a Wednesday!

Thomas of the Geological Society. Legend states that Merlin took the stones from Ireland to Stonehenge. This part of Wales was considered Irish in Merlin's day. Irish gold was carried by traders along the Golden Road in the early Bronze Age.

Refreshments
There are shops and a pub in Crymych.

St David's Cathedral

St David's

Outline
St David's – St Non's Well – St David's.

Summary
St David's has seen countless pilgrims. Tread the old paths from the city to St Non's Well and back to the cathedral.

Attractions
Tradition states that David, the patron saint of Wales, was born on the site now occupied by the ruins of St Non's chapel. The date may have been as early as 462 or as late as 520 and Non was his mother. David's father was Sant, Prince of Ceredigion. St David was born during a thunderstorm and the nearby St Non's Well is said to have sprung up during the event. Water was to become associated with St David. When he was brought for baptism to Aelfyw, Bishop of Mynyw, it is said that a spring miraculously appeared. The water from it cured the blindness of the monk who was holding the child. Later, the ascetic saint was to be known as the water-drinker, 'dyfrwr'.

Legend connects St David's with the Eastern Church, suggesting that David journeyed to Jerusalem and was consecrated Bishop by the Patriarch John III. Celtic Christianity has always had a direct link with the Holy Land, by-passing Rome, since the days when Joseph of Arimathea brought the young Jesus to Glastonbury. Pottery which probably contained communion wine has been identified as coming from the eastern Mediterranean. This is where the early Christian hermits, ascetics and monasteries were also to be found. Their ideas seemed to have reached David. The Welsh saint lived off bread and herbs, tilled the land himself without the aid of oxen, valued silence and spent long hours in devotion.

David's reputation grew after the Synod of Brefi. This may have been called to deal with a recurrence of the Pelagian heresy (Pelagius was a fifth century Ulsterman denounced as a heretic because he taught reincarnation and denied the doctrine of original sin). The event was also used to draw up a code of discipline for clergy and laity. The great crowd made it difficult for speakers to be heard. When David spoke the ground rose up to form a miraculous hill, while a dove rested on his shoulder. After his sermon, David was proclaimed Archbishop.

St David died on Tuesday, March 1st, 589. Forewarned of his death by angels, David's last words to his followers were 'be glad, and guard your faith and religion, and do the little things which you have heard from me, and which I have shown you'. March 1st became David's Saint's Day and pilgrims flocked here, with two pilgrimages to St David's being recognised as the equivalent of one to Rome. Three counted as one to Jerusalem.

Route 8

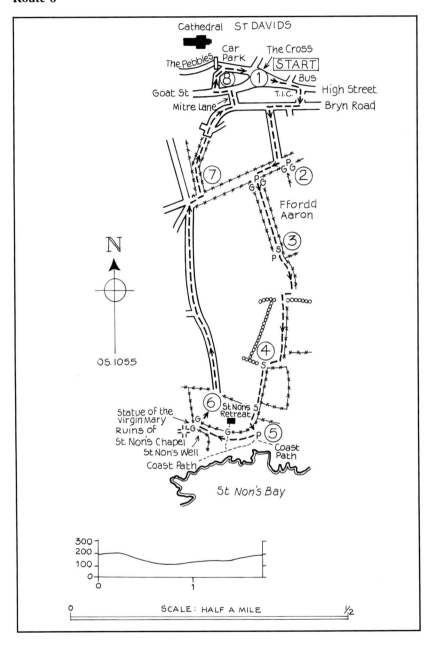

Cathedral   ST DAVIDS

The Pebbles   Car Park   The Cross   START   Bus

Goat St   T.I.C.   High Street

Mitre Lane   Bryn Road

Ffordd Aaron

N

OS. 1055

Statue of the Virgin Mary
Ruins of St Non's Chapel
St Non's Well
Coast Path

St Non's Retreat

Coast Path

St Non's Bay

SCALE: HALF A MILE

Route 8

St David's

Start

The medieval cross is the focal point of this village city, not far from the cathedral, car park, information centre and bus stop (GR SM753253).

Route

1. *Walk away from the cathedral, along the High Street. Pass the Information Centre on your right, then turn right as signposted for the public toilets. Go right at Bryn Road, ignoring a road opposite, but take the next turning on your left and continue to its end.*

2. *Turn right along the signposted path and take the first signposted turning on your left. This is Ffordd Aaron.*

3. *Go ahead over a stile and along the left-hand edge of a field. Go right in its corner and turn left through a gap. Walk along the left-hand edge of the next field and go right in its corner.*

4. *Turn left over a stile, follow the left-hand edge of the field to a stile in the corner ahead. Cross it, ignore the Roman Catholic Retreat on your right. Bear left through a gap and descend to the signposted junction with the Coast Path.*

5. *Turn right and soon fork right to pass the Retreat and its chapel on your right. Take the enclosed path in the corner ahead to reach St Non's Well, on your left. A gate next to it gives access to the ruins of St Non's Chapel. Continue through a small gate which has a statue of the Virgin Mary on its left. Follow the path to the Retreat's access lane.*

6. *Take the metalled lane inland towards St David's. Turn right when it is crossed by a track.*

7. *Turn left along the fenced path which emerges onto Bryn Road. Go left along Mitre Lane and turn left at Goat Street, soon passing the Farmers' Arms on your right.*

8. *Immediately after the pub, turn right along an alley to emerge near the fortified gateway overlooking the cathedral. Go right, past the car park, to return to the cross.*

Public Transport

St David's has a good weekday bus service to the railway station at Haverfordwest (no 340). There is also a good bus service (no 411) on weekdays to Fishguard.

Refreshments
There is a choice of places in St David's.

The eastern outlying stone, shaped like a seat, at Gors Fawr

Gors Fawr

Outline
Roadside west of Crymych — Stone Circle — Blaen-dyffryn — Adsofl-wen — Roadside west of Crymych.

Summary
An easy walk around a rough, boggy moorland but along good paths to one of the most important stone circles in Wales and to two enigmatic standing stones.

Attractions
The stones forming the circle are unimpressive for the major stone circle in Wales. The biggest stones (over six feet high) stand outside it, some 135 yards to the north. They are 45 feet apart and the outer (eastern) one is shaped like a seat. If an adult of normal size sits on it, the back of his or her head (perhaps relating to the pineal gland or 'third eye') is placed on a significant spot. Take a compass to it and the needle will swing about 30 degrees out of true. This stone has a magnetic area in a crucial position. Professor Thom calculated that the alignment formed by the two outlying stones marks the midsummer sunrise over Mynydd Preseli. The circle is formed by 16 fairly low stones and is about 72 feet in diameter. The stones are taller on the southern side of the circle with the tallest standing 4 ft 4 ins high.

Refreshments
Bring your own!

Test your compass at the eastern outlying stone

43

Route 9

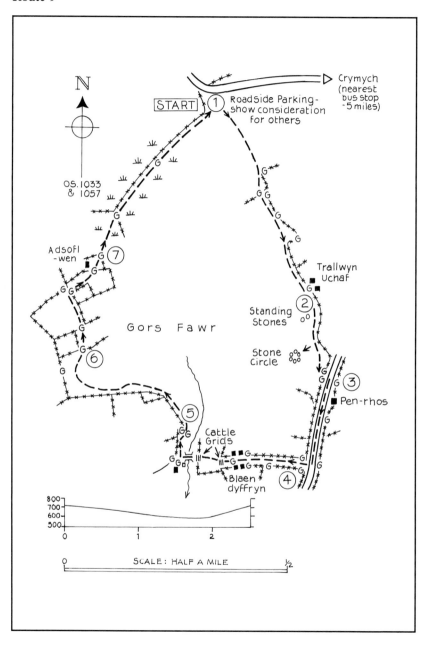

Route 9

Gors Fawr   2½ miles

Start

The walk starts about one mile west of Mynachlog-ddu, which lies four miles south-west of Crymych on the A478 Narberth to Cardigan road. Fork right after Mynachlog-ddu and follow the road across open moorland littered with stones. Stop when the road bears right and a farm track joins it on your left (GR SN132303).

Route

1. *Walk south, away from the road, and bear left at a fork. Reach a fence and go ahead with it on your left.*

2. *Visit the two outlying standing stones on your right, continue to the stone circle and reach a road through a small gate beside a fieldgate.*

3. *Turn right along the road, passing Pen-rhos on your left.*

4. *Turn right over a cattle grid along the access track to Blaen-dyffryn. Follow the track over two more cattle grids and bear right.*

5. *Continue with the fence on your left and the wild moorland on your right. As you approach a corner formed by a second fence, bear right towards a gate in the fence on your right.*

6. *Go ahead through the gate and along the left-hand edge of a small field to another gate. Continue through it and with a fence on your right to the next corner where you take the gate on your right and follow the path across the field to Adsofl-wen. Pass right of the farmhouse.*

7. *Follow the firm track over the boggy area, soon going through a gate ahead and walking with a fence on your left back to the start.*

Public Transport

The nearest bus stop is five miles to the east in Crymych (bus no 430 from Cardigan, tel. 0267 233 333 ext. 4333 for times) but you may find it worthwhile hiring a taxi.

Blue Peter tree in Haroldston Wood

Haroldston Wood

Outline
Broad Haven – Haroldston Wood – St Madoc's Church – Broad Haven.

Summary
A pleasant woodland walk is followed by a succession of fieldpaths and lanes back to Broad Haven.

Attractions
Broad Haven youth hostel is a good place to stay, having a family room and being next to the Information Centre. The woodland to its north is named after a local 'Harold Stone', which may commemorate a victory by the Saxon loser of the Battle of Hastings in 1066 (come on now, *everybody* knows that date) in earlier campaigns against the Welsh.

Haroldston Wood has the merit of consisting of native broadleaved trees, especially oak and ash. Planted in the 19th century as cover for hunting, the trees were coppiced until recently. Now managed by the National Park, an access agreement has opened up this woodland walk. Thousands of trees have also been planted, including those inspired by the appeal of the Blue Peter television programme.

The sheltered nature of the valley means that the trees can grow without being stunted by winds. They provide habitats for a variety of wildlife. In the sixth century, this valley was where a disciple of St David, St Madoc, came to pray and live as a hermit. He later became Bishop of Ferns. His ruined church stood above the northern end of the valley and was restored by the Victorians.

Tread softly and look out for badgers, foxes, rabbits, squirrels, field mice, shrews, voles, moles, stoats, weasels, polecats and minks. As you follow the final fieldpath down from Belmont to the lane, cast an eye over the sea to your right. As this is in the west, time your walk for sunset and a romantic evening.

Refreshments
There is a shop in Broad Haven.

Route 10

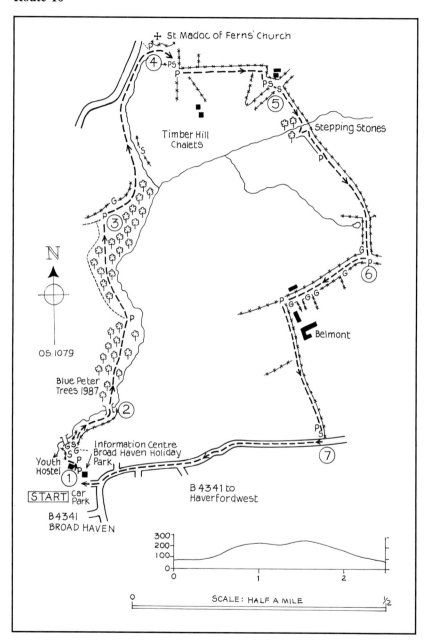

St Madoc of Ferns' Church

Timber Hill
Chalets

Stepping Stones

Belmont

N

OS.1079

Blue Peter
Trees 1987

Information Centre
Broad Haven Holiday
Park

Youth
Hostel

START Car
Park

B 4341
BROAD HAVEN

B 4341 to
Haverfordwest

SCALE: HALF A MILE

48

Route 10

Haroldston Wood   2½ miles

Start

To reach Broad Haven, follow the B4341 to the coast from Haverfordwest. The walk starts from the National Park Information Centre near the signposted car park and youth hostel in Broad Haven (GR SM864141).

Route

1. *Take the signposted Woodland Walk which runs north from the car park, passing the youth hostel on your left and the Information Centre on your right. Cross a stile, pass a footbridge which goes over a stream on your left and continue over a second stile to walk upstream to another footbridge.*

2. *Cross this footbridge, then bear right so that the stream is now on your right. Continue along the woodland path, passing trees planted in response to the Blue Peter appeal of 1987. Keep to the lower, right-hand, path at a signposted junction. Climb gradually through the wood.*

3. *At the next signposted junction, bear right along the path and keep the stream on your right until another signpost as you approach St Madoc of Fern's Church.*

4. *Turn right to pass the church on your left and follow the path to a stile. Go ahead as signposted, with a hedge on your left, to a gap on your left, where another signpost directs you to turn left. Continue with a hedge on your left through two fields and bear right to a signposted gap leading to a stile in the third. Cross it, a subsequent lane and another stile.*

5. *Walk with a hedge on your left down to a stream, which is crossed by stepping stones. Maintain your direction (bearing left a little to find the path immediately after the stream). Emerge at the edge of a field beside a signpost. Continue with a hedge on your left, pass a pond on your right and reach a lane.*

6. *Go right up the lane to its end and turn left along a headland path with the hedge on your left and a magnificent view over the bay towards Skomer Island on your right (a perfect place to admire a romantic sunset). Descend to a road.*

7. *Turn right along the road back into Broad Haven. Pass the Holiday Park and go right at the next bend to return to the car park, Information Centre and youth hostel.*

Public Transport

Bus no 311 connects Broad Haven with Haverfordwest on weekdays.

Enter Canaston Woods by crossing this stile at direction point 2

Canaston Woods

Outline
Link with Route 12 in Valley Road — Cilfoden Camp — Woodland Walk — Knights' Way — Cilfoden Camp — Link with Route 12 in Valley Road.

Summary
A splendid woodland walk leads to a broad, firm, track which forms part of the Knights' Way. This is ancient woodland, but the trees hide an even older Iron Age fort (Cilfoden Camp).

Attractions
Woodland paths are adventures in themselves. It is very important not to get lost, but you'd have a hard job to do that here, where the waymarking and signposting is excellent. Alien conifers have been planted, but much of this woodland is still home to native broadleaved trees, including beech and oak.

The ancient forest would have been primarily oak and hazel. It covered a large area and was a source of firewood and timber. One 120-gun 3-decked naval ship took the oaks of 75 acres of woodland in the 18th century, while fuel was also provided for the iron foundry at Blackpool Mill. The forest also provided cover for game and in 1834 the Baron de Rutzen of Slebech even planned to introduce wolves. Coppicing ensured a regular supply of wood throughout the 19th century and well into the 20th.

The Knights' Way is a waymarked trail of some nine miles between Amroth and Blackpool Mill. Its name harks back to the Middle Ages when members of the Knights Templar (founded in 1110 and dissolved in 1312) and the Knights Hospitallers of St John rode this way. The Hospitallers survived until the Dissolution and their badge was the white eight-pointed cross on a black mantle that now serves as the waymark for the Knights' Way. The Templars wore a red cross on a white mantle. They protected and provided for pilgrims, as well as fighting in the Crusades. The Hospitallers were stronger in this area, having a base at Slebech. The Templars were at Templeton.

Refreshments
See Narberth (Route 12).

Route 11

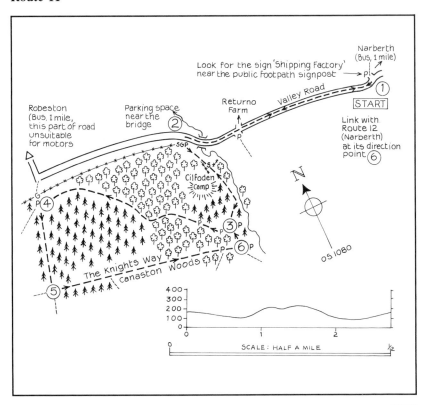

The signpost at direction point 4

Route 11

Canaston Woods   2¾ miles

Start

Link this walk with Route 12 (Narberth) at its direction point 6 to form a circuit of nearly six miles, or reach the linking point (at the sign 'Shipping Factory') by going down Valley Road, which is the lane on your right just after you cross Narberth Bridge, going south from Narberth with the A478 (Tenby road) (GR SN096143). Alternatively, shorten the walk by one mile by driving along Valley Road to a parking space near the bridge just before this route enters Canaston Woods (GR SN089143). If coming by public transport, there is an alternative bus stop (nos 322 and 381) at Robeston Wathen (GR SN084157).

Route

1. *Walk west, away from Narberth, along the Valley Road and pass the access track for Returno Farm on your right and a signposted path on your left. Follow the road across a bridge.*

2. *A short distance beyond the bridge, turn left over a stile beside a gate to follow a signposted path through Canaston Woods. Go ahead over another stile, reach the stream on your left and bear right up through the woods to a signpost.*

3. *Turn right and follow a clear woodland path which is waymarked with yellow arrows. It bears down to the perimeter fence, on your right, before reaching a signposted path junction near a gate.*

4. *Turn left up the signposted footpath which climbs into the wood.*

5. *Reach a broad track and turn left along it. This is signposted as the Knights' Way. Ignore two paths bearing right.*

6. *Turn left along a signposted path which soon brings you back to the route of your outward journey. Retrace your steps by forking right downhill.*

Public Transport

See Route 12 for details of buses to Narberth, then link the two routes. If walking the mile along the lane south from the bus stop at Robeston Wathen, that bus stop is served by nos 322 (Haverfordwest − Narberth − Carmarthen) and 381 (Haverfordwest − Narberth − Tenby).

A fragment of Narberth Castle

Narberth

Outline
Narberth – Narberth Castle – Valley Road – Link with Route 11 – Carding Mill Lane – Narberth.

Summary
Link this with the Canaston Woods walk (Route 11) to form a ramble of nearly six miles. Descend from the castle through fields to the valley road. Return along a delightful old green lane.

Attractions
Narberth is the Arberth of *The Mabinogion*, more correctly termed *The Four Branches of the Mabinogi*. This great body of Welsh literature was first written down during the Middle Ages, after being repeated by word of mouth over the preceding centuries. The memory of the bards was reliable for a people whose holy men were once the Druids, who chose to train their memories rather than commit words to writing. Arberth was the ancient capital of Dyfed and this is where Pwyll, prince of Dyfed held his chief court. After a feast, Pwyll went to the top of a mound known as Gorsedd Arberth (perhaps the site of Narberth Castle). There he received a vision of a lady on a white horse. This was Rhiannon and Pwyll soon proposed marriage to her. At a feast shortly before the wedding a rival suitor appeared who gained a boon from Pwyll. He, of course, asked for Rhiannon and Pwyll was now honour-bound to oblige him. Pwyll was distraught but Rhiannon urged him to bestow her upon his rival, 'lest dishonour come upon thee'. She was confident that the rival should never have her. Read the book to discover how she manages that!

Rhiannon did marry Pwyll in the end and bore him a son. The baby disappeared, however, with Rhiannon unfairly shouldering the blame. Forced to do penance because of others' lies, Rhiannon had to sit every day for seven years outside the gate of the court at Arberth, tell her story to everybody and offer to carry guest and stranger on her back to the court. Then the lost son turned up and Rhiannon was exonerated. Her son was to be known as Pryderi.

Later, now a widow, Rhiannon was bestowed upon Manawydan by Pryderi. Read about this in the Third Branch. Once again it features the mound known as Gorsedd Arberth. Could this be the castle mound? The Normans are known to have had a castle here by 1116, when it was burnt by the Welsh. It was rebuilt, perhaps on a different site, by the 13th century. Very little remains today. The drovers who bought cattle in Narberth market for driving to England have gone too. Once a major route centre and the scene of a Rebecca Riot, Narberth is now a hospitable, unspoilt town whose community spirit is expressed by the volunteers who care for its railway station.

Route 12

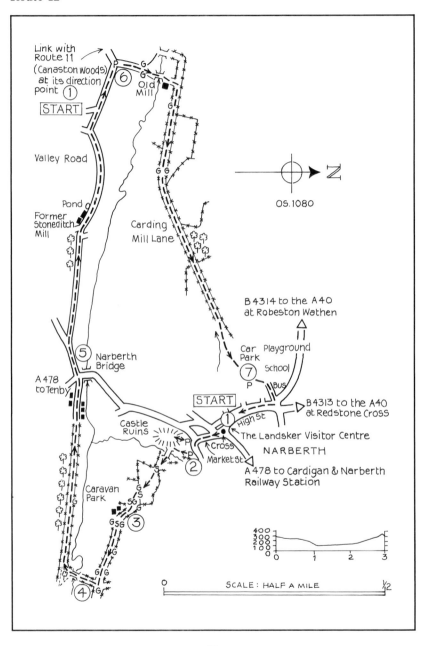

Link with Route 11 (Canaston Woods) at its direction point (1)

START

6

Old Mill

Valley Road

OS.1080

N

Pond

Former Stoneditch Mill

Carding Mill Lane

B 4314 to the A40 at Robeston Wathen

Car Park   Playground

School

5   Narberth Bridge

7

Bus

P

A 478 to Tenby

START

1   High St

B 4313 to the A40 at Redstone Cross

Castle Ruins

P

Cross

The Landsker Visitor Centre

2

Market St

NARBERTH

Caravan Park

A 478 to Cardigan & Narberth Railway Station

3

4

SCALE : HALF A MILE   ½

56

Route 12

Narberth   3 miles

Start

The Landsker Visitor Centre is in the centre of Narberth, forming an island at the southern end of the High Street. A signed car park is near the bus stop at the northern end (GR SN110146).

Route

1. *Face the entrance to the Visitor Centre, with the steps going up to its first floor door. Fork left, pass a cross and go down Market Street. Divert, as signposted, to visit the castle ruins and with your back to the castle, go right.*

2. *Turn right down a signposted path which runs below the castle mound on your right. Turn left to cross a footbridge and go ahead to a stile in the corner. Cross it and maintain this direction through two more fields and over stiles beside gates.*

3. *Reach a farm access track and go ahead along it to a crosstracks. Turn right down towards a bridge over a stream.*

4. *Cross the bridge and bear right, then turn right to follow the track along the valley. This passes a caravan park on your right and acquires a metalled surface. Go ahead across the A478, passing Narberth Bridge on your right.*

5. *Take the road ahead until it forks, then bear right along the valley road. Pass an old mill with its pond on your left and reach a signposted track junction on your right, which is where Route 11 (Canaston Woods) starts.*

6. *Continue this route by turning right down to the stream. Cross it and climb up to an old green lane (Carding Mill Lane). Go right along this back into Narberth.*

7. *From the car park, go ahead to the main road and turn right down the High Street back to the Visitor Centre.*

Public Transport

Narberth has a station on the railway from Pembroke to Carmarthen (the junction is at Whitland, some trains continue to Swansea, Cardiff or London – there is a Sunday service). The no 381 bus links Narberth with Haverfordwest and Tenby on weekdays.

Refreshments
There is a choice of places in Narberth.

The gateway to St Peter's church, Lampeter Velfrey

Lampeter Velfrey

Outline
Lampeter Velfrey – The Landsker Borderlands Trail – Lampeter Velfrey.

Summary
This is a relaxing stroll from a tranquil village surrounded by evidence of our prehistoric ancestors. Turn off a lane to follow the waymarked Landsker Borderlands Trail and pass ancient standing stones before returning back down another lane to St Peter's Church.

Attractions
Dyfed County Council are to be congratulated for their promotion of the Landsker Borderlands Trail. Old paths have been cleared, signposted, waymarked and had necessary gates and stiles put in place. A circular route of some 60 miles, this is a holiday in itself. Start the circle at Whitland, where there is a railway station and walk south-west, to include this section near Lampeter Velfrey, to reach the Daucleddau Estuary at Lawrenny. Turn north to Canaston Bridge and continue to Efailwen, then turn east to visit Llanboidy before going south back to Whitland. A leaflet describing the trail is available from the Landsker Borderlands Visitor Centre, The Town Hall, Narberth, which is where Route 12 (Narberth) starts. Alternatively, contact SPARC (South Pembrokeshire Partnership for Action with Rural Communities), The Old School, Station Road, Narberth, Dyfed, SA67 8DU, tel. 0834 860965.

'Landsker' is a word of Norse origin, meaning 'frontier'. It is an imaginary line dividing the Welsh (north) and English (south) speaking parts of Pembrokeshire. The southern part of Pembrokeshire has long been known as 'Little England beyond Wales' but the border was never defined and was fought over. This area, for instance, counted as English, but the name of the house passed on this route is Welsh (Coed-y-Ffynnon, meaning 'woodspring'). Lampeter is derived from the Welsh word 'Llanbedr', meaning 'the sacred enclosure dedicated to Peter'. Velfrey is the anglicised form of 'Efelffre', the old Welsh name for this commote or area.

This must be an ancient settlement, with the remains of Stone Age chambered tombs suggesting people lived here 5,000 years ago. The standing stones seen from this walk are more prehistoric monuments, to go with local Bronze Age barrows and Iron Age forts. The ringwork thrown up to the north of the church may date from the 12th century, when Giraldus recorded that his uncles Hywel and Walter (the son of the beautiful Nest) were given the territory and, perhaps, fortified it. St Peter's Church was substantially rebuilt in the 13th century, suggesting the place was of some importance. The cross in the churchyard dates from the 14th century, while the celtic cross to be seen at the churchyard's eastern end is fairly modern. Visit the church but allow time too for the playground which stands just across the road from the church gates.

Route 13

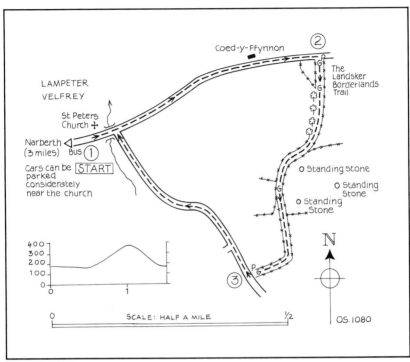

Take this gate on the Landsker Borderlands Trail

60

Route 13

Lampeter Velfrey   1½ miles

Start

Lampeter Velfrey is about 3 miles east of Narberth. Cars can be parked considerately near the church (GR SN155144).

Route

1. *Face the church gate (with children's swings at your back) and go right. Follow the road across a bridge and pass a turning on your right (down which you will return). Pass Coed-y-Ffynnon on your left.*

2. *Turn right up the signposted Landsker Borderlands Trail. Look out for the standing stones in the second field on your left. Emerge from this old green lane at a road.*

3. *Turn right down the road back to Lampeter Velfrey, going left at the junction to retrace your steps over the bridge to the church.*

Public Transport

You'll probably conclude that it's better to walk the extra three miles each way from Narberth to Lampeter Velfrey, but it is possible to bus to the start of this walk on Thursdays by taking the no 381 bus from Tenby (currently at 10 am). As the return bus doesn't leave until 1.56 pm, you might as well stroll into Narberth for a bus back to Tenby.

A waymark post

Refreshments
Bring your own!

Cross the 'doggy' stile to enter the Deer Park

Deer Park

Outline
National Trust car park − Coast Path − Overlooking Skomer Island − Wooltack Point − Coast Guard Lookout − 7th Century Cross − National Trust car park.

Summary
A glorious headland walk overlooking Skomer Island.

Attractions
Dogs on leads are welcome on this walk and there is even a special 'doggy' stile giving them admission to the Deer Park. This tip of land was cut off by an Iron Age earthwork or rath (implying an Irish influence) long before the stone wall was built around 1800 and the keeping of deer was considered (there is no evidence that they actually were kept here). Proof that this spot was special in prehistoric times is furnished by the Celtic cross, dating from the seventh century, now in the wall near the Information Centre. Skomer Island, which can be seen across Jack Sound beyond the smaller Midland Isle, has more ancient remains. It is formed of hard resistant volcanic lava, at least 400 million years old. Seabirds and seals may be seen. Thousands make the crossing to Skomer every year to enjoy the birds, especially the puffins. The landing stage in Martin's Haven is the departure point for the seasonal boat service to Skomer Island.

Refreshments
Bring your own!

Looking across Jack Sound to Midland Isle and, beyond it, Skomer Island

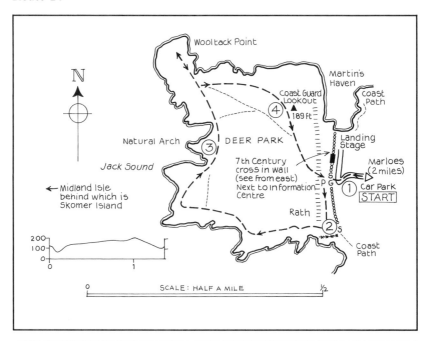

The view from near direction point 2, looking east

Route 14

Deer Park   1½ miles

Start

Take the B4321 out of Haverfordwest, and take the right turn for Marloes. The walk starts from the National Trust car park on your left-hand side at the end of the road about two and a half miles west of Marloes (GR SM761090).

Route

1. *Go left along the road to where it bends left, then right (to serve the landing stage). Go straight ahead to cross a stile beside a gate in the wall of the Deer Park. Turn left to walk south with the wall on your left and the rampart of the rath on your right.*

2. *Reach the southern coast where the Coast Path comes over a stile on your left. Go right to walk with the sea on your left around the headland.*

3. *Notice the natural arch, opposite Midland Isle (across Jack Sound, with Skomer Island beyond). Proceed to Wooltack Point and continue near the northern shore, keeping the sea on your left. Climb to the Coast Guard Lookout.*

4. *Descend to the stile beside the gate to return to the eastern side of the wall. Divert left past the Information Centre to see the seventh century cross set in the wall. Retrace your steps to return to the car park.*

Public Transport

The nearest bus stop is over two miles away in Marloes (for nos 315 and 316 from Haverfordwest, on Tuesdays, Fridays and schooldays only).

Looking towards Milford Haven from the coast path

66

St Ishmael's

Outline
St Ismael's — Coast Path — Monk Haven — St Ishmael's.

Summary
This is a different side of the Pembrokeshire Coast Path, near the oil refinery at Milford Haven. This is a distant feature, however, as you traverse the usual exciting clifftop path. Descend to Monk Haven and walk inland up a wooded valley to an important Celtic Christian church.

Attractions
The bay (Lindsway Bay) immediately on your left when you reach the Coast Path is where Prince Charles first set foot on Welsh soil in 1955. The natural harbour of Milford Haven is of immense strategic importance, so it comes as no surprise to find this coast was fortified. German aircraft dropped magnetic mines by parachute into these waters during the Second World War. One of these sank the 6,426 ton merchant ship *Dakotian* on November 21st, 1940, when her cargo partly consisted of Christmas puddings. The crew were saved, although one sailor swam ashore from a point about half a mile south of Monk Haven and went back to his family in Milford Haven without telling the authorities not to bother searching for him.

The watch tower above Monk Haven is a folly which was built in 1860. The road from here to St David's provided pilgrims with a safer route to St David's than the sail around Pembrokeshire's coast. St Ishmael was a disciple of St David and succeeded him as Bishop (or Archbishop?) in 589. There was a teaching monastery in St Ishmael's and the church still has a special spiritual quality to it.

Refreshments
There is a pub and a shop in St Ishmael's.

Route 15

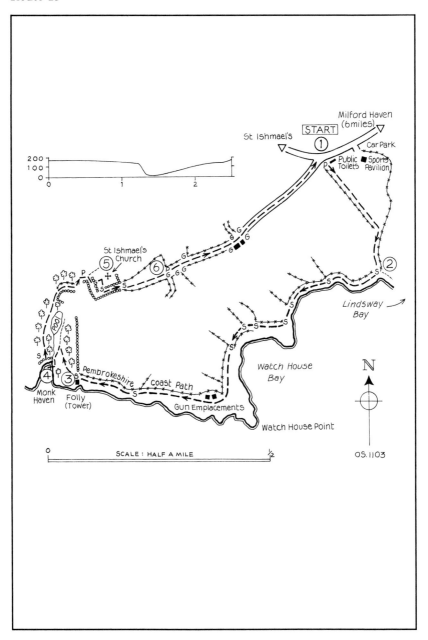

Route 15

St Ishmael's   2½ miles

Start

St Ishmael's is about six miles west of Milford Haven. The walk begins on the eastern edge of the village, where it may be possible to park near the sports pavilion (GR SM839072).

Route

1. *Face the public toilets, in the north-western corner of the sports field, and pass them on your left as you go ahead along the signposted public footpath which runs along the right-hand edge of the sports field. Bear right through a gap in the far corner and continue with a hedge on your left to a stile giving access to the Coast Path.*

2. *Go right along the Coast Path, keeping the sea on your left. After one mile take a bar stile in an old estate wall ahead, above Monk Haven, passing a tower built as a folly on your left.*

3. *Bear right inland and down through woodland to a path junction where you turn sharply left back towards the sea. Reach the beach at Monk Haven and turn right along it.*

4. *Turn right through a gap in the wall. Ignore the Coast Path as it bears left over a stile. Go ahead up the wooded valley and pass a pool on your right. Pass what seems like an old walled garden on your right, bearing right, then left, to pass a house and emerge at St Ishmael's Church.*

5. *From the church porch, go straight ahead up the graveyard to a slate stile in the wall. Cross it and turn left along the enclosed path. Emerge over a stile and go ahead with a hedge on your right.*

6. *Take the gate in the corner to go ahead along a track which becomes a road and leads back to the start of this walk.*

Public Transport

There are buses to St Ishmael's from Haverfordwest (nos 315 and 316) on Tuesdays and Fridays only.

Go down these steps to St Govan's Chapel

St Govan's Head

Outline

Car park − Coast Guard Lookout − St Govan's Chapel and Well − Car park.

Summary

This is an easy stroll along a surface which would enable the use of a pushchair. You do have to go down steps to see St Govan's Chapel and Well, however.

Attractions

St Govan's Chapel is a very special place. Luckily it is isolated and access is down a daunting flight of steps, so it has retained its spiritual nature. Only come here if you can respect it. Avoid popular times and find it possible to meditate in this powerful place. My companion and I both experienced significant dreams after doing so. St Govan no doubt had many. Perhaps it is the rocky fissure behind the altar that is the spot to sleep.

An information board (see page 71) at the car park tells you all about St Govan and this remote chapel. Read it. There is no mention of a connection between St Govan and King Arthur's Sir Gawain (also identified as Gwalchmai). Tradition does suggest that this worthy knight did become a hermit, however. As a son of Gwyar, he was a nephew of King Arthur. There is a Castell Gwalchmai (Walwyn's Castle) near Haverfordwest, from where this courteous knight once ruled part of Dyfed. St Govan also left his name in the part of Glasgow which now contains Ibrox stadium. Whatever his origin, he ended up here. Pirates may have thought it worthwhile capturing him to obtain a ransom, but he escaped by hiding in the cleft in the rock which is now behind the altar which contains his bones. He died here in 586, probably on March 26th, which is his Saint's Day.

There are about 74 steps down to the chapel but try counting them and see if all your party can agree on the answer. There used to be a well in the floor near the entrance to the chapel. St Govan's Well is below and has run dry. Tap the large rocks outside to see which one is the 'Bell Rock'.

Tragedy came to the rocks below St Govan's Head on November 16th, 1880, when the 600 ton cargo steamship *Ailsa* was wrecked here. Everybody on board was lost, including seven passengers. The ship was on a voyage from Bristol to Glasgow with a cargo of iron hoops, lead piping and tanned hides. Ten bodies were washed ashore and are buried in the churchyard at Bosherston.

Refreshments

Bring your own!

Route 16

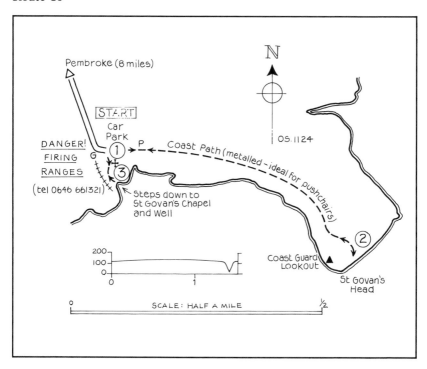

St Govan's Chapel

Route 16

St Govan's Head   1½ miles

Start

Reach St Govan's Head by following the B4319 south from Pembroke. Park in the car park at the end of a road which runs south from the B4319 at Sampson Cross. This road may be closed on certain days. Telephone 0646 661321 to check (GR SR967930).

Route

1. *Facing the sea, go left along a metalled track which is ideal for pushchairs and is signposted as the Coast Path. Keep the sea on your right until you reach the Coast Guard Lookout on St Govan's Head.*

2. *Retrace your steps to the car park, this time with the sea on your left. Turn left down steps to visit St Govan's Chapel and Well.*

3. *Return up the steps to the car park.*

Public Transport

The nearest bus stop is one mile away in Bosherston and the service (nos 364 and 365) runs infrequently on Tuesdays only plus schooldays from Pembroke.

73

St Govan's Well

Useful information

Approximate mileage of each walk from Haverfordwest via main roads.

Route	Haverfordwest
1	33
2	20
3	18
4	23
5	24
6	16
7	24
8	16
9	22
10	6
11	11
12	10
13	13
14	14
15	6
16	18

Looking north towards the natural arch and Wooltack Point on the Deer Park
(Route 14)

Routes in order of difficulty

None of these walks would be strenuous to an experienced walker. The following grading is made in the context of a Family Walks book and is done with the fairly active six or seven year old in mind.

Easy Walks

Route 5 — Careg Sampson (4 miles)
Route 8 — St David's (1¾ miles)
Route 9 — Gors Fawr (2½ miles)
Route 12 — Narberth (3 miles)
Route 14 — Deer Park (1½ miles)
Route 16 — St Govan's Head (1½ miles)

Moderately difficult

Route 1 — St Dogmael's (2 miles)
Route 3 — Carregwastad Point (3 miles)
Route 6 — Pont Faen (2½ miles)
Route 10 — Haroldston Wood (2½ miles)
Route 11 — Canaston Woods (2¾ miles)
Route 15 — St Ishmael's (2½ miles)

More strenuous

Route 2 — Pwll Deri (1½ miles)
Route 4 — Carn Ingli (3½ miles)
Route 7 — Foeldrygarn (1¾ miles)
Route 13 — Lampeter Velfrey (1½ miles)

The memorial on Carregwasted Point (Route 3)

The coast path north of Trevine (Route 5)

Public transport

Your holiday begins when you board the train or bus. Let your children enjoy the thrill of public transport to gain access to the countryside. This will help the environment and safeguard the future of these public transport routes. Instead of being isolated from the land you pass through by the width of a car window, you can become part of it by mixing with the locals who depend on the bus or train. Don't be afraid of taking their seats! They'll welcome your support for their vital service. Relying on public transport will also prevent you from bringing all you need from home. You will contribute more to the local economy by buying necessities in local shops. Don't think this will preclude camping. There are several campsites which are close to bus stops or railway stations so that you don't have to carry tents and sleeping bags far. We camped not far from the bus stop in St David's and near the railway station at Manorbier. The youth hostels are also often a reasonable distance away from public transport and don't require the carrying of lots of equipment. Many have family rooms now. Trains run west from Swansea to Pembroke, with useful halts at Narberth, Kilgetty, Saundersfoot, Tenby, Penally, Manorbier and Lamphey. Another line goes to Haverfordwest and Milford Haven, while a third runs to Fishguard Harbour (for the Rosslare ferry). Buses run to many places and there are free timetable booklets available in Tourist Information Centres and by post from the Highways & Transportation Dept, Dyfed County Council, Llansteffan Road, Carmarthen, Dyfed, SA31 3LZ. Tel. 0267 233333, extension 4333.

Tourist information addresses

Pembrokeshire Coast National Park, County Offices, Haverfordwest, Dyfed, SA61 1QZ. Tel. 0437 4591. There are National Park Information Centres at Broad Haven, Haverfordwest, Kilgetty, Newport, Pembroke, St David's, Saundersfoot and Tenby. There is a Tourist Information Centre at Fishguard.
The Landsker Visitor Centre, Town Hall, Narberth, Dyfed. Tel. 0834 860061.
SPARC (South Pembrokeshire Partnership for Action with Rural Communities), The Old School, Station Road, Narberth, Dyfed, SA67 8DU. Tel. 0834 860965.

Gors Fawr stone circle (Route 9)

Wet weather alternatives

Completely or partly under cover. It may rain in Pembrokeshire, so it is useful to know where to go if it's too wet for a walk. The following list is not comprehensive and current tourist information should be consulted. It is arranged by its proximity to each walk.

Walk 1: Y Felin, St Dogmael's; Cardigan Aquarium.

Walk 2: Tergwnt Woollen Mill.

Walk 3: Wolfscastle Pottery.

Walk 4: Cilgwyn Candles.

Walks 5 & 6: Llangloffan Farmhouse Cheese Centre.

Walks 7 & 9: Felin Geri Watermill; National Coracle Centre.

Walk 8: Oceanarium; Marine Life Centre; Cathedral; Bishop's Palace.

Walk 10: Haverfordwest Castle Museum, Haverfordwest Swimming Pool.

Walks 11, 12 & 13: Landsker Visitor Centre; Oakwood Park.

Walks 14 & 15: Milford Haven Museum.

Walk 16: National Museum of Gipsy Caravans, Pembroke.

A woodland walk (Route 6)

THE FAMILY WALKS SERIES

Family Walks on Anglesey. Laurence Main. ISBN 0 907758 665.

Family Walks in Berkshire & North Hampshire. Kathy Sharp. ISBN 0 907758 371

Family Walks around Bristol, Bath & the Mendips. Nigel Vile. ISBN 0 907758 193.

Family Walks around Cardiff & the Valleys. Gordon Hindess. ISBN 0 907758 541.

Family Walks in Cheshire. Chris Buckland. ISBN 0 907758 290.

Family Walks in Cornwall. John Caswell. ISBN 0 907758 55X.

Family Walks in the Cotswolds. Gordon Ottewell. ISBN 0 907758 150

Family Walks on Exmoor & the Quantocks. John Caswell. ISBN 0 907758 460.

Family Walks in South Gloucestershire. Gordon Ottewell. ISBN 0 907758 399.

Family Walks in Gower. Amanda Green. ISBN 0 907758 630.

Family Walks in Hereford and Worcester. Gordon Ottewell. ISBN 0 907758 207.

Family Walks on the Isle of Wight. Laurence Main. ISBN 0 907758 568.

Family Walks in North West Kent. Clive Cutter. ISBN 0 907758 363.

Family Walks in the Lake District. Barry McKay, ISBN 0 907758 401.

Family Walks in Mendip, Avalon & Sedgemoor. Nigel Vile. ISBN 0 907758 41X.

Family Walks in the New Forest. Nigel Vile. ISBN 0 907758 606.

Family Walks in Oxfordshire. Laurence Main. ISBN 0 907758 38X.

Family Walks in the Dark Peak. Norman Taylor. ISBN 0 907758 169.

Family Walks in the White Peak. Norman Taylor. ISBN 0 907758 096.

Family Walks in South Derbyshire. Gordon Ottewell. ISBN 0 907758 614.

Family Walks in South Shropshire. Marian Newton. ISBN 0 907758 304.

Family Walks in Snowdonia. Laurence Main. ISBN 0 907758 320.

Family Walks in the Staffordshire Peaks and Potteries. Les Lumsdon. ISBN 0 907758 347.

Family Walks around Stratford & Banbury. Gordon Ottewell. ISBN 0 907758 495.

Family Walks in Suffolk. C.J. Francis. ISBN 0 907758 649.

Family Walks around Swansea. Raymond Humphreys. ISBN 0 907758 622.

Family Walks in the Teme Valley. Camilla Harrison. ISBN 0 907758 452.

Family Walks in Three Peaks & Malham. Howard Beck. ISBN 0 907758 428.

Family Walks in Mid Wales. Laurence Main. ISBN 0 907758 274.

Family Walks in the North Wales Borderlands. Gordon Emery. ISBN 0 907758 5909.

Family Walks in Warwickshire. Geoff Allen. ISBN 0 907758 533.

Family Walks in the Weald of Kent & Sussex. Clive Cutter. ISBN 0 907758 517.

Family Walks in Wiltshire. Nigel Vile. ISBN 0 907758 215.

Family Walks in the Wye Valley. Heather & Jon Hurley. ISBN 0 907758 266.

Family Walks in the North Yorkshire Dales. Howard Beck. ISBN 0 907758 525.

Family Walks in South Yorkshire. Norman Taylor. ISBN 0 907758 258.

Family Walks in West Yorkshire. Howard Beck. ISBN 0 907758 436.

The publishers welcome suggestions for further titles in this series; and will be pleased to consider manuscripts relating to Derbyshire from new or established authors.

Scarthin Books of Cromford, in the Peak District, are also leading second-hand and antiquarian booksellers, and are eager to purchase specialised material, both ancient and modern.

Contact Dr D.J. Mitchell, 0629-823272.